Beautifully Broken

Chelle Ellard

BookLeaf
Publishing
India | USA | UK

Presentation by *BookLeaf Publishing*

Web: www.bookleafpub.com

E-mail: info@bookleafpub.com

ISBN: 9789363303447

First edition 2024

ACKNOWLEDGEMENT

To Jim, the love of my life who held me up and never let me fall. Your unconditional love and support were always the net beneath me, giving me the courage I needed to work through my trauma and become the woman I was meant to be. And to Jack & Kathleen Stell, without whom I would have never stood a chance. My deepest gratitude to all of you, thank you for believing in me and for never letting go.

PREFACE

During moments of isolation and pain, writing served as my constant companion. It embraced my deepest fears and harbored my darkest secrets, providing an escape from a life marked by tragedy and suffering. Though vulnerable and lost, being able to put my thoughts on paper was something I could control. It was something that could not be taken from me, and it was at times, the only friend I had on my side. Through the written word, I found the strength to blossom anew, and want you to know that you can too.

May my words wrap around you like a warm embrace, providing comfort, encouragement, and a reminder that you're not alone. In brokenness, there lies a unique beauty that deserves to be embraced with open arms. Wear your pain like an unbreakable shield, allowing your vulnerability to transform into a powerful armor capable of withstanding any challenges thrown your way.

Life Sentence

Not all love is good or happy, and neither are
some men
A false promise of security and fairytales were
all he vowed
Pulled into him by a web of lies, only to be
baited and trapped
Held tightly by his grip, at his mercy to feed off
of whenever the urge struck
Deceptive and destructive are who and what my
husband became
The wolf in sheep's clothing hiding among the
flock, waiting to attack me
A once vibrant girl full of naivety and dreams
withered away with each blow
Slowly he degraded every ounce of pride and
self-worth,

A sinister game where only he could be the
winner, he played me so well
Carefully crafted methods of torture he perfected
over time,
Guaranteed to break even the strongest of souls,
ensuring total submission
Battered and helpless, I longed for reprieve, for
mercy, for death
Muffled screams often pierced the silence on
many endless, dark nights
Barely hanging on to life I thought, if I could
just make it until the sun rose
And it always did but nothing ever changed,
every day became a repeat
A brutal cycle of tearing me down, emotionally
and physically stripping me of all I was
My body becoming unrecognizable from daily
abuse
My mind fractured and no longer functioning
except out of the need to simply survive
I am one of the lucky ones who got away with
my life, only it wasn't me anymore
I am forever conditioned to react with fear, to
anticipate pain and punishment
Even though I know I don't deserve it and it
won't happen to me again
Never knowing what will affect me or when the
panic attacks will come on

Leaves me feeling like I am still a prisoner to
him, that he still owns me
His death brought me no comfort, no
reassurance that he couldn't get to me anymore
And his ghost often still haunts me in my dreams
even though I know it isn't real
Learning to trust a man once felt impossible but
I am being shown that it isn't
I look forward to the day that I can close my
eyes and not see him and no longer hear his
voice
Not all love is good or happy, and neither are
some men,
I vow to live with hope-filled eyes ensuring that
he won't win

My Abyss

Amidst the unwelcome embrace of solitude, my
soul finds itself submerged.
Waves of darkness surge relentlessly, taking
their toll.
In the ebb and flow of isolation's tide, I am
consumed.

Loneliness engulfs me, penetrating every crevice
within, leaving no space untouched.
The merciless passage of time erases remnants
of happiness, smiles, and joy,
leaving behind a void that seems
insurmountable.

Cherished friendships, now lost to the
ruthlessness of time's hands,
Echoes of youth fade into the distance.
Regret and memories intertwine, a bittersweet
refrain,
Guiding my steps on this solitary path I must
remain.

A future shrouded in shadows, cold and bleak,
Alone I tread, my destiny spoken.
Acceptance cloaks me, embracing the decree of
fate,
A solitary soul, forever liberated.

A Familiar Existence

You knew where to find me again
In the distant past, I am certain our souls had
entwined. Separated only by time and space,
everything about us familiar—what I had been
longing to find again. It didn't matter the
physical attributes made us strangers because the
spiritual realm reminded us of who we already
were, what we already knew.
At my weakest and most trying moments, I
despaired I had suffered a damage so great that
nothing could make me whole again. Yet, there
you were, steady and strong, willing to brave the
war I had barely survived, to sacrifice yourself,
to carry my worn body and spirit until I could
stand on my own.

Your gentle caress cradled the broken pieces of
me, retrieving every splintered part, breathing
love and life back into every crevice. Amazed by
your miracles and in awe of your presence, there
is nothing now that terrifies me, nothing now I
should fear. Apprehension and doubts subsided
with each day that passed us, slowly melting
away into an abyss below us, allowing us to rise
above it.
A constant state of bliss and gratitude has
replaced the darkness that once enveloped me. I
no longer obsess over trying to understand why I
am worthy of such salvation and adoration; I
accept it with grace and humility hoping to
never lose grasp of this heaven we exist in.
Whether for only a moment or for an eternity,
our souls are tethered, as are our hearts. Nothing
shall sever the ties that bind us, nothing can
distract or delay us from what we already are
and will be. I am yours as you are mine, I owe
you everything now and forever.

Passive Aggression

Regretful lament pours from deep within a place
I am ashamed exists
Only recently acquiring the knowledge of my
severe dysfunction, I am vilified, I am ashamed
Dysmorphia of the mind only serves to be my
demise, my petulance has become absurd
A portrayal of false persona, incapable of
self-acceptance and insecurities, inhospitable
verbalization of my fears manifests so cruelly, so
berating
Subjecting others to my selfish eruptions, I bare
my transparency by projecting an embarrassing
view into the window to my true soul

In truth, I am aware of my genuine ego—an
abolished and banished pariah, crying out for
recognition, weeping to be seen
All the while, I understand the depths of my
uncomfortable nature, yet I'm still too afraid to
acknowledge what I know I can no longer ignore
Cowardly deceit my forte, a manipulator who
has mastered her tirade
If only I hadn't lied to myself, would I have a
chance to change who I have resolved to
despise?

A Godless World

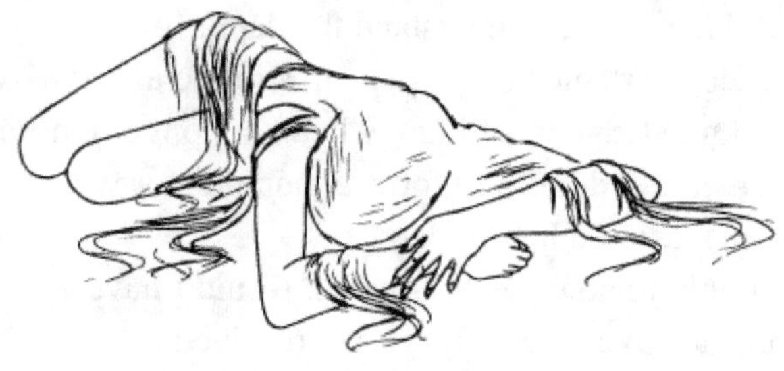

Pieces of my broken body lay scattered upon the floor
My dignity crucified, shattered remnants of my soul
Desperately clinging to a thread of hope,
begging to be called home.

Gathering what remains of life, I question worth
and purpose, undeserving of a gentle touch to
soothe the agony of his wrath
Trembling hands too worn from the fight,
weakened arms struggle to hold on, finding
nothing of promise beyond this moment....the
darkest night upon my soul

Only silence grants me peace, a quiet escape
inside my mind
The only place his grasp can't reach, sheltered
from the violence, preserving the one piece left
of me. Untouched and unharmed, purity of my
being activated the moment the rest of me died

Too frightened to cry out, too beaten down to
rise above
Unsettling reality of mistakes I've made,
resulting in this hell
Isolated from all light, forbidden to feel alive
Reprimanded without cause, his blackened eyes
pierce through the veil of God

Sinking ever so slowly into this sea of fire and
hell, swallowing my existence, digested by the
belly of the Devil

A thousand prayers unanswered by a God who
cannot exist, whose cruel and unjust prophecies
have dug my grave and sealed my fate

She has weathered

Written words that speak to me, exposing my
invisibility and for a moment becoming a voice.

A portal that opens, giving breath to the altars
who reside inside me, yet I remain unaware.

Allowing each to surface, facilitating a stage on
which to present themselves.

All things kept hidden now overspill like an
ocean that swallows me, I am the vessel and the
sea is my tears.

Thrashing from stern to bow, my titanic mind
sinking, slipping, I am tilted as I remain.

A weakened, raw throat forces out the pain. A
scream that could pierce glass, shattering the air
around me.

Hear me, find me, save me.

Then suddenly, raging waters calm, the sun
breaks just above; my voice has been found

An escape from the storm that has weathered my
soul, my words freeing, unscripted and flowing,
urging me to heal.

From trauma to thought, remembering all—
recall, reprieve, release..letting go of its hold.

TBI

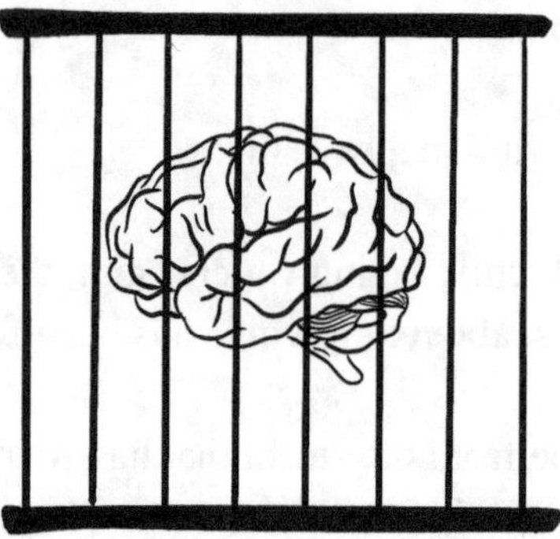

Tell me in a way I understand Momma, said her little boy so sweet
I know you say you're sick but you look good as new to me
How do you hide the Band-Aids that cover up your brain?
Never have I seen them and I've looked almost everyday
Sometimes I see you crying as you're curled up on the floor,
I don't know how to help you so I stand silent at your door
Daddy says not to bother you but doesn't tell me why,
It's hard to watch you struggle, when I see how hard you try
I hate when you look confused and roam aimlessly about,

It's scary when you get angry, I don't like it
when you shout
Maybe when I'm all grown up, your brain won't
hurt no more,
I can kiss it better! Like you did when I was four
I hope you won't forget me like the things you
can't remember,
Like January starts the year and ends it with
December
I promise that I'll be here to help you find your
way,
Tomorrow will be better Momma, everything
will be ok

Domestic Violence

She longed to live
But after him,
Death was welcomed

The Truth

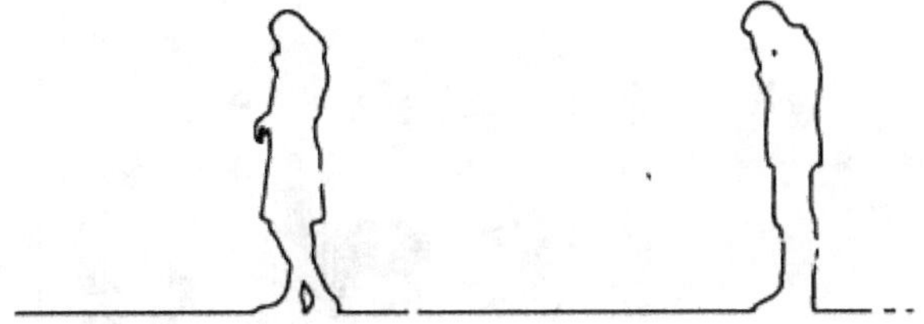

I will never hurt you.
I promise not to let you down.
I'm sorry, that's a lie.

She wasn't born a Masterpiece

A rainbow of colors spreads across the pages of her life, a complexity of hues and shades
Each tint and dye reminiscent of time and emotions, sacrifice and tragedy
In the infantry of her artwork, the depths cannot be seen yet
Yet through the years and fine mistakes, one begins to visualize her convalescent enrichment
Dark tones of deep and bleeding reds stain the page with her worries and rage
Complemented with a softness of tranquility and peace, bright yellows and faint blues that overlap one another

Flecks of black and streaks of green showcase
her jealous envy at times,
While violet wisps that flutter like butterfly
wings, unveil the true desires of her heart
This colorful mural, landscape of her life
Holds all that has broken her, all that has made
her whole
This portrait is her, what makes her beautiful, a
Remington of modern times

A Battered Woman

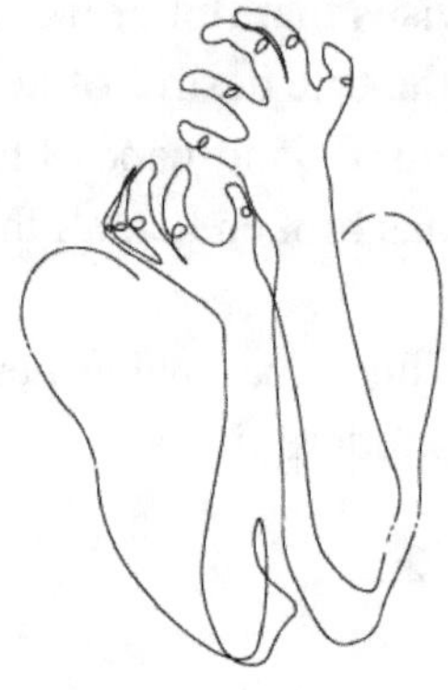

Foundation unshaken
Tragedy not an obstacle
I am a survivor

She Weeps

If you should wake tomorrow and find me fast
asleep,
be gentle not to wake me, for my broken heart
still weeps.

Allow me one more moment, as it's you I'm
dreaming of,
the way we used to be, the way we used to love.

Your tenderness surrounds me, every touch feels
like the first;
let me live here in this moment, to wake now
would be the worst.

Caress my aching heart the way your hands have
always done,
wrap yourself around me, in case today is our
last one.

Whisper if you can, a promise that our love will
last,
reassure me that this nightmare I am living will
soon pass.

If you should wake tomorrow and find me fast
asleep,
be gentle not to wake me, for my broken heart
still weeps.

Aged

A polished master of mistakes, enlightenment
beholds me
I stand breathless in the face of adversity—a
beautiful disaster I am indeed

Shattered

A once-brilliant mind is now broken
All I can say remains unspoken
Distant and weathered, hard to recall
Seldom are words found, if at all
Scattered memories fade,
Edges of the mind become frayed
Flickers of moments, though not mine
Unable to find, the more I try
The damage is too great to repair
All that I have lost feels so unfair
Leaving me empty, void of hope
Defeated, unable to cope
Silently screaming, this my fate
Salvage my soul, not too late

Just thought you should know

As time passes by, the hurt in your heart will become numb—not better, just numb. You will adapt to a life with that hole inside your chest because you have to, not because you want to or should.
The tears will come often and at the most inopportune places, but let them fall so that you don't. To live is to grow, but to grow, we must also let go, even when we cannot. Forgive the things that keep you awake at night when you are alone with nothing but your thoughts. I believe that we will all find forgiveness in the end, but take a chance to live like that while you are still here.

In grief there is no time; sometimes it creeps by
while other times, you have no idea where it
went. So grasp each moment to be the person
you wish others could be for you right now. My
arms wrap around you like a shield, I am sorry
that you now know the depth of what a loss can
do to us. It changes you completely, and you will
never be the same again.
You age, become humble and find a love for
things and people that you forgot were there.
Embrace everything that you can and know that
you will see him again someday, we all will. I
love you more than words...just thought you
should know.

The Other Woman

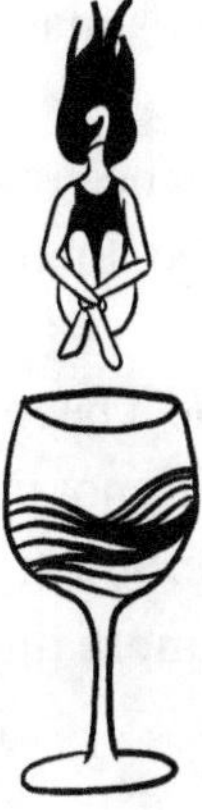

She has taken the place where I once used to
stand,
She has stolen my kisses and taken your hand
It is her that you turn to when comfort is what
you need
And it's she who fulfills your desires and greed

She became your good mornings, and now your
good nights
She was subtle yet swift and provoked all of our
fights
You promised you'd leave her, that she wouldn't
stay long
You gave me your word, said you knew it was
wrong

Do you care what she's done? Can't you hear all
my cries?
Can you face me like a man and quit telling me
lies?
A decade of love has been washed all away
Replaced and rejected, there isn't much left to
say
I give up; I get it, she's been hard to resist
Between her and I, it's not me that you missed
It's clear you are over me, it is her you choose
I deserved so much more than to be replaced by
your booze

Hateful regret

Long ago forgotten remnants of a promised life
innocence, intention, stolen dreams whisked
from my soul
bitterness resides now where love and hope once
lived,
blackened rose-colored glasses that see the
world with hate and fear
my cold, concrete heart too damaged to forgive
trust betrayed by those too close, regret for
letting them in
silent nights invaded by the voices in my head
battling a war that rages on eternally, defeated
by the win
stand alone beside myself, what have I done this
time?

yes, mistakes do bear the ignorance of ego and
desires
praying for salvation, I wonder if there's hope
for me?
begin again or resolve to let go, it's time that I
must choose
to do it better if I had the chance, so many things
I'd change
lessons learned, though hard ones, are all that's
left now in my grave

I despise you

Love is a battlefield
though I am not your war
your destruction smells of death,
your intention smells of fear
a coward where a man once stood

Transitioning

Tomorrow I'll be shedding the only me I've known, releasing all I used to be in spite of how I've grown
Stepping out of my old skin and into something new, the new me that I will become will bid the old me Adieu
The ceiling of potential has fallen at my feet, I'm anxiously awaiting the old and new to meet
Two strangers finally stand, nose to nose and eye to eye—hello to the new me, and to the old, I say goodbye

Paper Time Machines

Handwritten collections composed
or addressed are much more than
just scriptures or thoughts,
Scribbles and notes of scattered
ideas, memoirs of battles fought

Paper that's folded and perfectly
creased holding onto the
secrets of many,
A vessel for words one might like
to say whether seldom
and few or plenty

Reminders of moments we would
like to relive, and of those, one
might wish to forget
Stories unfold like scenes in a film,
your imagination running as
wild as you'll let

A forgotten first love and the way
that you felt, you swore it was
together forever
Whirlwind affairs and stories of
lust and of things that you
swore you would never

Reminiscent hysterics of yesterdays
gone, evoking the same
fits of laughter
An echo of sorts to a time we
once were, a replication of
happily ever after

Pages with faded crayons and
smiles, a few misspelled
words never mattered
A mother's reunion any time it feels
lonely, now that her small
family is scattered

Timeless encounters of those who
have passed, each letter can
bring them to life
Bring a grown man to tears while he
falls to his knees as he reads
the last words of his wife

One man's hello and another's
goodbye, a dear John that
still holds its pain
Each stain like a scar, each stain
a reminder, catching tears as
though they were rain
Cherish each note, letter and
card; each is a key
that unlocks
a timeline of sorts, a preservation
of life, paper time machines
kept in a box

My Kintsugi

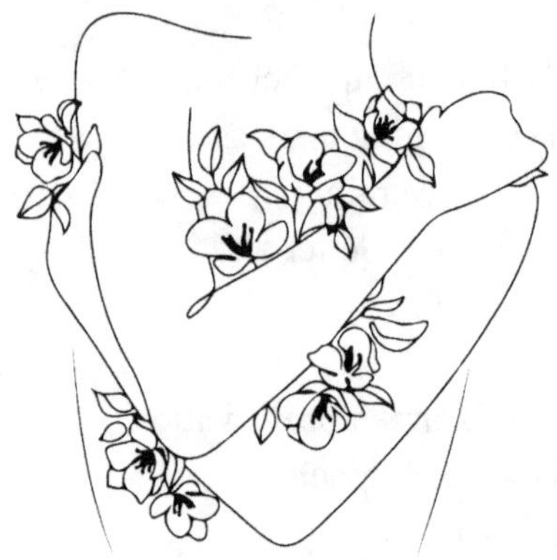

Scars that mark my body from the wars that I
have won,
Receipts from every battle fought without
bullets or a gun
Wounds no longer open, getting stronger as they
heal,
Remnants of the way I used my body as a shield
Crevices and cracks I once thought showed me
as weak,
The physical manifestation of what happens
when you don't speak
With age and time comes wisdom and a better
sense of self
An understanding that my body is the bank of
my life's wealth

www.ingramcontent.com/pod-product-compliance
Lightning Source LLC
Chambersburg PA
CBHW061728130726
47996CB00006B/2550